Ecosystems
Wetlands

Galadriel Watson

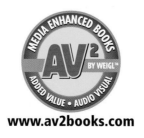

www.av2books.com

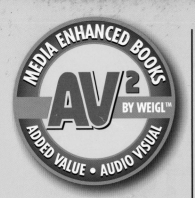

AV² provides enriched content that supplements and complements this book. Weigl's AV² books strive to create inspired learning and engage young minds in a total learning experience.

Your AV² Media Enhanced books come alive with...

Audio
Listen to sections of the book read aloud.

Key Words
Study vocabulary, and complete a matching word activity.

Go to **www.av2books.com**, and enter this book's unique code.

Video
Watch informative video clips.

Quizzes
Test your knowledge.

BOOK CODE

L651341

Embedded Weblinks
Gain additional information for research.

Slide Show
View images and captions, and prepare a presentation.

AV² by Weigl brings you media enhanced books that support active learning.

Try This!
Complete activities and hands-on experiments.

... and much, much more!

Published by AV² by Weigl
350 5th Avenue, 59th Floor
New York, NY 10118
Website: www.av2books.com   www.weigl.com

Library of Congress Cataloging-in-Publication Data

Watson, Galadriel Findlay.
  Wetlands / Galadriel Watson.
    p. cm. -- (Ecosystems)
  Includes index.
  ISBN 978-1-61690-643-6 (hardcover : alk. paper) -- ISBN 978-1-61690-649-8 (softcover : alk. paper)
  1. Wetland ecology--Juvenile literature. I. Title.
  QH541.5.M3W335 2011
  577.68--dc22
                        2010050991

Printed in the United States of America in North Mankato, Minnesota
1 2 3 4 5 6 7 8 9 0 15 14 13 12 11

052011
WEP37500

Project Coordinator Aaron Carr
Design Sonja Vogel

Contents

What is a Wetland Ecosystem?

Saltwater marshes fill with water each time the tide comes in and empty again when the tide withdraws.

Earth is home to millions of different **organisms**, all of which have specific survival needs. These organisms rely on their environment, or the place where they live, for their survival. All plants and animals have relationships with their environment. They interact with the environment itself, as well as the other plants and animals within the environment. These interactions create an **ecosystem**.

Wetlands are places where the soil is drenched with water at least part of the year. Wetland water can come from nearby lakes, rivers, streams, or oceans. It can also come from rainfall, snowmelt, or **groundwater**. Wetlands can contain fresh water or salt water, which is either still or slow moving.

There are four types of wetlands. Bogs are areas of soggy ground filled with moss or partly decomposed plant matter called peat. Fens are peat-filled areas that support a wide variety of plant life, such as grasses and wildflowers. Marshes are wetlands that do not contain peat. They are home to many types of grasses. Swamps are similar to marshes, but they contain trees and shrubs instead of grasses.

Eco Facts

Cranberries grow in bogs and marshes. Store-bought cranberries are grown in bogs made by humans.

It may take as long as 10,000 years for a bog or fen to form. It takes only a few days for humans to destroy a bog or fen.

Many animals, including amphibians, birds, fish and shellfish, insects, mammals, and reptiles, live in wetlands. The combination of plants and animals makes wetlands some of the most productive ecosystems in the world. The plants and animals of the wetlands are uniquely adapted to their waterlogged homes.

Levels of Organization in Wetland Ecosystems

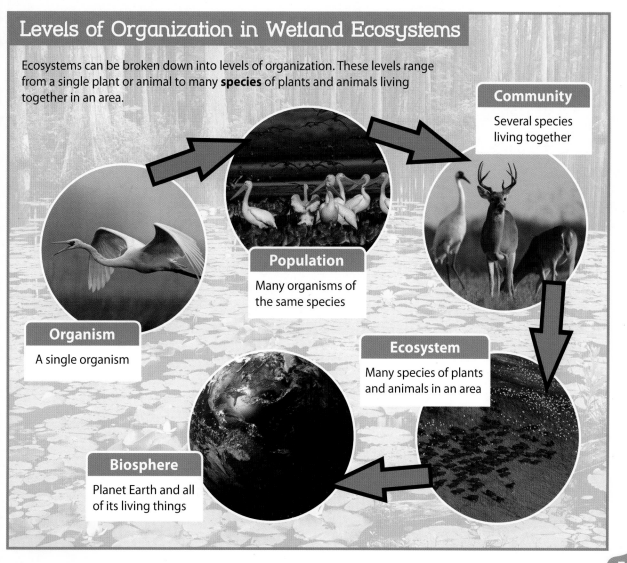

Ecosystems can be broken down into levels of organization. These levels range from a single plant or animal to many **species** of plants and animals living together in an area.

Community
Several species living together

Population
Many organisms of the same species

Organism
A single organism

Ecosystem
Many species of plants and animals in an area

Biosphere
Planet Earth and all of its living things

Where in the World?

Bogs are characterized by acidic water covered by a thick mat of partly decomposed plant material.

Every continent except Antarctica has wetlands. Wetlands cover an area between 2 and 3.3 million square miles (5.3 and 8.6 million square kilometers) around the world. This is between 4 and 6 percent of the world's surface area, or about the same size as Brazil. About 65 percent of the world's wetlands are located in **tropical** and **subtropical** regions. Other wetlands are found in cooler areas, including polar regions.

Most bogs and fens are located in the Northern Hemisphere. About 10,000 to 2.5 million years ago, **glaciers** covered many areas in the Northern Hemisphere. When the glaciers retreated, they scraped out depressions in the land. These depressions became ponds after they filled with rainwater or melting snow. Over time, many of these ponds—found in Canada, the northern United States, northern Europe, and northern Asia—became bogs or fens. Bogs and fens are also found in warmer, wetter parts of the world, such as Great Britain, Indonesia, Africa, and South America.

Marshes are located in shallow lakes and streams throughout the world. They are also found in the **deltas** of most of the world's great rivers, including the Amazon River in Brazil, the Mississippi River in the United States, and the Nile River in Egypt. Swamps are also located throughout the world near slow-flowing rivers, in areas of low-lying land, and along ocean coasts.

Many parts of the world are known for their wetlands. One area in Great Britain is called the Fens. This area is a fen of about 400 square miles (1,036 sq. km). That is larger than the size of New York City. The best-known wetlands in the United States include the Everglades in Florida and the Great Dismal Swamp in North Carolina and Virginia. The Everglades cover an area of about 4,000 square miles (10,400 sq. km). This is almost twice the size of Delaware. The Great Dismal Swamp once stretched about 2,000 square miles (5,200 sq. km). Today, this wetland has been drained to 172 square miles (445 sq. km).

Eco Facts

Twenty-four percent of the world's wetlands—more than 490,350 square miles (1,270,000 sq. km)—are located in Canada.

More than 4 million prairie potholes, a type of marsh, are found in the prairie regions of Canada and the United States.

The American flamingo lives in the wetlands of Central and South America.

Wetland ecosystems are found on most of the world's continents. This map shows where the world's major wetlands are located. Find the place where you live on the map. Do you live close to a wetland area? If not, which wetland areas are closest to you?

Legend

- Wetlands
- Ocean
- River

Scale at Equator

0   1,000   2,000   3,000 miles

0   1,000   2,000   3,000 km

N

ARCTIC OCEAN

Prairie Potholes, Canada and United States

Mackenzie River Basin, Canada

Hudson Bay Lowlands, Canada

NORTH AMERICA

NORTH ATLANTIC OCEAN

Everglades

Location: Florida, United States
Size: 4,000 square miles (10,400 sq. km)
Fact: This subtropical saw grass marsh region covers much of southern Florida with shallow, slow-moving water. More than 350 bird species are found in the Everglades, along with populations of alligators, bobcats, river otters, and many species of snake, lizard, and turtle. Water in the Everglades is usually less than 1 foot (30.5 centimeters) deep.

Mississippi River Basin, United States

Amazon River Basin, Brazil

SOUTH AMERICA

SOUTH PACIFIC OCEAN

Magellanic Moorland, Argentina

Pantanal

Location: South America
Size: 54,000 to 81,000 square miles (140,000 to 210,000 sq. km)
Fact: Pantanal is the world's largest freshwater wetland ecosystem. It is located in the floodplain of the Paraguay River and its tributaries. Annual floods bring fish in increased numbers. During the dry season, Pantanal is home to 656 bird species and more than 100 mammal and reptile species.

Wildfowl and Wetlands Trust

Location: United Kingdom
Size: 4,940 acres (2,000 hectares)
Fact: The Wildfowl and Wetlands Trust is made up of nine wetland preserves throughout England, Northern Ireland, Scotland, and Wales. It is home to one of the world's largest collections of waterfowl. More than 3,000 birds from 200 species are found here. Notable bird species include all six flamingo species and the Hawai'ian goose.

ASIA

Western Siberian Lowland,
Russia

Lake Chad Basin,
Chad

PACIFIC OCEAN

EUROPE

Nile River Basin,
Egypt and Sudan

AFRICA

EQUATOR

SOUTH ATLANTIC OCEAN

INDIAN OCEAN

AUSTRALIA

Congo River Basin

Location: West-central Africa
Size: 73,360 square miles
(190,000 sq. km)
Fact: The Congo River Basin is home to one of the largest wetlands in the world. It contains the Ngiri-Tumba-Maindombe, the world's largest protected wetland. This 25,300-square mile (65,700-sq. km) site contains the largest body of fresh water in Africa. This area is the only habitat for a type of chimpanzee called a bonobo.

ANTARCTICA

Wetland Climates

If wetlands disappear due to global warming, many unique plants, including the water lily, will disappear as well.

Wetland ecosystems experience many climates depending on their location in the world. Bogs and fens are most common in colder areas. Marshes and swamps can be found in any climate.

Global Warming

Some scientists are concerned that **global warming** will affect wetlands. Many human activities increase the amount of heat-trapping **greenhouse gases**, including carbon dioxide and methane, in the atmosphere. This increase causes Earth's climate to continually warm in a process called the greenhouse effect. Hotter, drier summers mean wetlands have less water to keep them moist. Pollutants that run into wetlands are more concentrated in the remaining water. Global warming is also causing glaciers to melt faster and ocean waters to expand—causing ocean levels to rise. If ocean levels rise too much, many wetlands will drown.

Carbon Stores

Bogs store carbon in peat. If global warming causes bogs to dry out, the peat will decay or burn in a wildfire. Carbon stored in these bogs will be released into the air, increasing the greenhouse effect.

Water Flow

Wetlands are a vital part of Earth's flow of water. They act as sponges, absorbing rainwater, snowmelt, surface water, groundwater, and floodwaters. During dry times, this water slowly seeps away from the wetlands, keeping groundwater, nearby streams, and other bodies of water at normal levels. Wetland plants protect shores and banks from wearing away over time. Their roots hold the soil in place and slow the force of currents and waves.

Eco Facts

Canada's bogs hold about 137 billion tons (124.3 billion tonnes) of carbon. This is equal to 26 years of worldwide carbon emissions from the use of **fossil fuels**.

By reducing use of poisonous chemicals such as pesticides, the effects of global warming on wetlands can be reduced.

Floods

During floods, wetlands absorb runoff and precipitation. This helps reduce the amount of flooding downstream. If flooding continues, wetlands in lower areas play two central roles. First, they hold and store some of the floodwaters. Second, their vegetation helps slow the movement of floodwaters.

Cleaning Power

Wetlands are sometimes called "Earth's kidneys" because they help clean water. When water flow slows down in wetlands, **sediment** sinks to the bottom. Plants and microorganisms absorb **minerals** and pollutants in the water. When the water seeps out of the wetlands, it is much cleaner. Wetlands are so efficient at cleaning water that they perform the same task as wastewater treatment facilities.

Tidal flats are muddy areas that fill with water and empty with changing tides. The nutrient-rich mud of tidal flats is home to a variety of life, including algae, crabs, and worms.

Types of Wetlands

Alligators are often found among floating vegetation in many wetland ecosystems.

Bogs

Bogs begin as small lakes or ponds that are fed almost entirely by precipitation. Most plants cannot grow in this water because it does not have many minerals. However, sphagnum moss grows well in these conditions. Sphagnum moss grows along the banks of the wetlands. Gradually, the moss spreads over the water's surface. Sphagnum moss makes the water **acidic** and low in oxygen. When pieces of the moss die, the presence of acid and the lack of oxygen in the water slow the decaying process. The moss and its remains form a layer of peat on the water's surface. Over time, the peat thickens, and pieces sink to the bottom of the bog. Eventually, peat fills all the water.

Fens

Like bogs, fens begin as small lakes or ponds that are fed by precipitation. However, fens also receive some groundwater or surface runoff. Fens have more minerals and less acid in their water. They can support plant life. However, peat still accumulates. If enough peat builds up, the fen can be cut off from its supply of mineral-rich water and become a bog.

Marshes

Marshes receive many more minerals than bogs or fens. In marshes, plant matter decays. It does not become peat. Marshes have waterlogged, rich soils that make them the perfect home for various types of grasses. Marshes can contain fresh water or salt water. Freshwater marshes develop in areas of shallow water along the edges of lakes, rivers, or other bodies of water. Some freshwater marshes form in low-lying areas that are wet only part of the year. Saltwater marshes are found along coasts where rivers or streams run into oceans or seas.

Eco Facts

When peat layers grow very thick, they become strong enough to support trees. These wooded bogs are often called muskegs.

In 1950, two people discovered the body of a man in a bog in Tollund, Denmark. The bog had preserved the man's body, hair, and clothes for more than 2,000 years.

Swamps

Like marshes, swamps have rich soils. They do not fill with peat, and they contain fresh water or salt water. However, grasses do not grow in swamps. Instead, woody plants, such as shrubs and trees, grow in these areas. Movement causes water to fill with oxygen. Swamps move very slowly or not at all, so they do not contain much oxygen. This lack of oxygen means dead plant matter cannot completely decay. Instead, plant matter remains partially decayed in the water. This causes swamp water to look dark, like coffee or black tea.

The egret uses its long legs to wade into wetlands in search of food.

Wetlands are important to the plants and animals that depend on them for food, water, and shelter. In fact, wetlands are often called "nurseries of life" because they support so many species. Wetlands make up 5 percent of the land in the United States, but they are home to 31 percent of the country's plant species.

Producers

Grasses and other plants found in wetlands act as producers for other organisms in the ecosystem. Producers absorb energy from the Sun and convert it into usable forms of energy such as sugar. Producers make this energy through a process called **photosynthesis**. Producers found in wetlands include mangrove trees, many types of grass, such as saw grass, and algae.

Primary Consumers

The animals that rely on producers as a food source are called primary consumers. When a primary consumer feeds on a producer, the energy made by the producer is transferred to the primary consumer. Examples of primary consumers found in wetland ecosystems include insects, such as the periwinkle snail, mammals, including deer and beavers, and some waterfowl, such as geese.

Wetland Energy Pyramid

The transfer of energy in an ecosystem begins with producers and moves up the energy pyramid to the tertiary consumers. Organisms at each level of the pyramid receive energy from the organisms in the level below them.

Outside of the pyramid are the decomposers. They break down the dead and decaying organic matter left behind when plants and animals die. For this reason, decomposers receive energy from organisms in all levels of the energy pyramid.

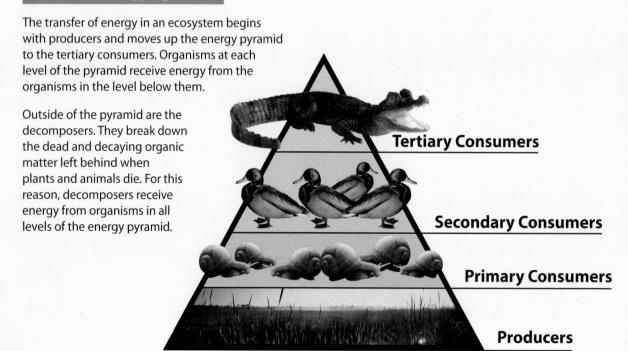

Tertiary Consumers

Secondary Consumers

Primary Consumers

Producers

Wetland Food Web

Another way to study the flow of energy through an ecosystem is by examining food chains and food webs. A food chain shows how a producer feeds a primary consumer, which then feeds a secondary consumer, and so on. However, most organisms feed on many different food sources. This practice causes food chains to interconnect, creating a food web.

In this example, the **red line** represents one food chain from the grass, goose, and bald eagle. The **blue line** from the mangrove tree, beaver, and caiman form another food chain. These food chains connect in other places. The beaver feeds on grass as well, and the goose also eats the mangrove tree. This series of connections forms a complex food web.

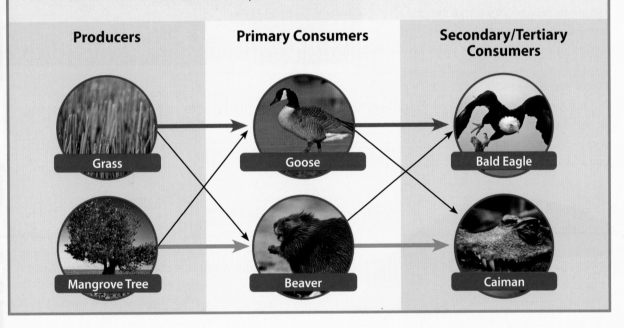

Producers	Primary Consumers	Secondary/Tertiary Consumers
Grass	Goose	Bald Eagle
Mangrove Tree	Beaver	Caiman

Secondary and Tertiary Consumers

Secondary consumers feed on both producers and primary consumers. In wetlands, secondary consumers include insects, such as dragonflies, mammals, including muskrats, and waterfowl, such as ducks. Alligators and other large carnivores are called tertiary consumers. Tertiary consumers feed on secondary consumers.

Decomposers

Fungi, such as mushrooms, and many types of bacteria live in wetland ecosystems. These organisms are called decomposers because they eat dead and decaying **organic** materials. Decomposers speed up the process of breaking down dead organic materials and releasing their **nutrients** into the soil. These nutrients are then absorbed by the roots of trees and other plants.

Plants

Sphagnum Moss

Found in bogs, sphagnum moss is the collective name for about 200 species of moss. Sphagnum moss is also called peat moss or bog moss. It has large dead cells in its stems and leaves, which absorb and hold water. As the moss fills with water, it stops air from passing through to the water below. For this reason, the water below is anoxic, or lacks oxygen. The moss also absorbs any minerals in the water and replaces them with acid. The water in which the moss grows is low in minerals. These factors prevent the growth of bacteria and fungi, the two organisms responsible for decay. Since there is no bacteria or fungi in bogs, the moss does not decompose. Instead, it accumulates until the water is filled with peat and the area becomes a bog.

Sphagnum moss contains a green cover of live moss with an underlayer of decaying plant matter.

Carnivorous Plants

Carnivorous plants thrive in bogs. These plants have developed a unique way to obtain the nutrients they need to survive. They eat insects and spiders. The pitcher plant has leaves shaped like a juice pitcher. To catch insects, it secretes a sweet nectar near the mouth of the pitcher. When an insect tries to eat the nectar, it becomes tangled in the pitcher's stiff, downward-pointing hairs. Inside the plant, the insect drowns in a pool of rainwater. The plant then uses special **enzymes** to digest the insect.

The venus's-flytrap is just one of the carnivorous plants found in bogs.

Mangroves are able to take in oxygen through special breathing roots.

Mangroves

Mangrove swamps are home to thick mazes of mangrove trees. Located along tropical seacoasts, mangrove swamps receive a mixture of fresh and salt water—an ideal situation for these water-loving trees. The tree roots and stems protrude from the ground like stilts. Fish and shrimp lay eggs under the mangroves. Other animals live in the treetops, never touching the water below. The trees also shelter inland areas from severe storms such as hurricanes and tidal waves.

Eco Facts

There are about 600 known species of carnivorous plants, which are also called insectivorous plants.

Sphagnum moss can grow up to 12 inches (30 cm) high. The moss usually grows close together, forming a soft, spongy mat.

Sphagnum moss can hold up to 20 times its weight in water. For this reason, gardeners often spread the moss around plants to keep them moist in hot, dry climates.

Peat can be dried and used for fuel. It has also been used in diapers, as bedding, and as surgical dressings.

When peat hardens from pressure underground, it turns into coal.

The common, or red, mangrove tree grows to about 30 feet (9 meters) tall. The black mangrove can grow up to 69 feet (21 m) tall.

Land-loving Animals

Birds

Many birds use wetlands as permanent homes, breeding or nesting grounds, or rest stops on long migrations. Some of these animals are especially suited to living in wetlands. For example, herons and egrets have long, pointed bills and long necks that allow them to reach and take food, such as fish and crabs, underwater. Their long legs allow them to wade in shallow water, while their wide-spreading toes help them walk on muddy soil. Some birds have special lungs that inflate like balloons so they can float on the water's surface. Their lungs deflate so that they can dive below the water.

The emperor goose breeds in the wetlands of the far north.

Mammals

Many mammals visit wetlands for food and water. Some have adapted to live their entire lives in these areas. For example, muskrats and otters have webbed feet for swimming. Beavers also have webbed feet and a flattened tail, which they use to steer in the water. The beaver has a large liver and large lungs, allowing it to hold its breath underwater for more than 15 minutes. Beavers can close their ears and nostrils when diving. They can also cover their eyes with a membrane that allows them to see underwater. Beavers have musk glands that produce oils to waterproof their fur.

The sika deer is a mammal that is often found in marshy areas.

Eco Facts

Beavers can create their own wetlands. Beaver dams flood large areas, turning meadows into marshes and forests into swamps.

The Suncoast Seabird Sanctuary in Florida is the largest bird sanctuary and hospital in the United States. The sanctuary takes in up to 10,000 injured birds each year. The sanctuary contains an emergency center, a surgery center, and both indoor and outdoor recovery areas for birds. The birds that come to the sanctuary are released back into the wild upon recovery.

North America's prairie pothole region is called a "duck factory" because about half of all the continent's migratory birds—including ducks— stop at these wetlands during their yearly migrations.

Crocodiles have pointed snouts, whereas alligator snouts are more rounded.

Reptiles

Reptiles, such as lizards, snakes, and turtles, depend on wetlands. Crocodiles live in swamps and marshes. Their long, thin bodies and muscular tails help crocodiles move quickly through the water. Their nostrils, eyes, and ears are located on the top of their head, so they remain above water while the rest of the body is underwater. Nostril and ear flaps stop water from entering the crocodile's head. A membrane closes over the eyes so that the crocodile can see underwater. Crocodiles have webbed feet that allow them to swim easily, as well as walk on soft ground.

The carpet snake lives in the dense reed beds of Australia.

Water-loving Animals

Amphibians

Amphibians are cold-blooded animals that spend part of their lives in the water and part on land. Frogs and salamanders, for example, begin their lives as aquatic tadpoles with gills and tails. As they grow, they pass through **metamorphosis** to become land-dwelling animals that breathe air through their skin and lungs. Many amphibians use wetlands as breeding grounds or permanent homes.

Young red-spotted newts are bright red with black-bordered spots on their back.

Fish and Shellfish

Marshes are home to many types of fish and shellfish. Some spend their entire lives in marshes. Others visit only to spawn, or lay eggs, and nurse their young. The young fish are safer in marshes than in open water because they can hide from predators among the marsh plants. Some fish species found in freshwater marshes include bass, carp, and pickerel. Fish species found in saltwater marshes include flounder, sea trout, and striped bass. Saltwater marshes also host many species of shellfish, including clams, crabs, oysters, and shrimp.

In order to reproduce, salmon travel hundreds or thousands of miles (km) to return to the stream or river where they were born.

Frogs live on every continent except Antarctica. Most species live in the world's tropical regions.

In very cold areas or in times of drought, many amphibians burrow into the mud to stay moist.

Fiddler crabs live in saltwater marshes and mangrove swamps. Male fiddler crabs have a huge front claw, which they hold in their other claw in the same way a person would hold a violin.

Insects

Water bugs live in watery wetland areas. In addition to eating other insects, water bugs eat small fish, salamanders, and tadpoles. To remain on top of the water's surface, water striders, or pond skaters, rely on special claws and a covering of short hairs. Both water boatmen and backswimmers have long, flat, hairy back legs they use like oars to move through the water. Water scorpions live on the bottom of ditches and muddy ponds. They hide in dead plant matter, waiting to ambush their prey.

Monarch butterflies frequent prairies, meadows, and wetlands.

Wetlands in Danger

Many wetlands have been destroyed to make way for businesses, farms, houses, and roads. Wetland animals have become **endangered** as a result. Global warming has caused some wetlands to dry up. Non-native plant and animal species have invaded other wetlands. Some wetland animals are captured as pets. Other wetland animals are hunted as food.

When too many minerals, such as phosphorous and nitrogen, enter a wetland, a large amount of algae grows in the water. As algae decompose, they consume the water's oxygen. Not enough oxygen remains in the water for other aquatic plants and animals to survive. Many die. This condition is called hypoxia.

In the United States, nearly half of all threatened or endangered species live in wetlands permanently or use wetlands for some part of their lives. Worldwide, about 45 types of waterfowl—birds that rely on watery places such as wetlands—are near extinction. In the early 1900s, egret feathers were used to make hats. Due to high demand, the bird was hunted almost to extinction. When the hunting stopped, the egret population increased. In Hawai'i, there was once a large Hawai'ian, or Nene, goose population. By 1949, fewer than 30 of these birds remained due to overhunting. Some Hawai'ian geese were bred in facilities to help increase their population. In 1992, 2,200 birds were released into the wild.

Timeline of Human Activity in Wetlands

The San Francisco Bay area contains about 849 square miles (2,200 sq. km) of wetland ecosystems. Over the next 200 years, this ecosystem is reduced to about 48 square miles (125 sq. km).

A new law requires all waterfowl hunters of ages 16 and older to purchase a Migratory Bird Hunting Stamp. The money from these stamp purchases is added to the National Wildlife Refuge System. This is one of the first examples of dedicated funding for wetlands conservation.

Biologists Samuel P. Shaw and C. Gordon Fredine publish "Wetlands of the United States: Their Extent and Their Value to Waterfowl and Other Wildlife." This publication establishes the term "wetland" and outlines the importance of protecting these ecosystems.

1800s	1899	1934	1946	1956	1969

The United States Congress passes the Rivers and Harbors Act. It is the first federal water pollution act in the country. The laws of this act are later expanded in the 1972 Clean Water Act.

British conservationist Sir Peter Scott establishes a 418-acre (169-hectare) protected wetland site along the River Severn in Gloucestershire, England. Protecting this wetland ecosystem plays an important role in saving the Hawai'ian goose from extinction.

A legal battle to build an airport in the Florida Everglades ends when President Richard Nixon votes against the proposal. The United States Department of the Interior produces the first environmental impact statement in an effort to stop the airport development.

Today, 106 countries have joined the Ramsar Convention, which states they must preserve important wetlands as nature reserves. More than 1,900 Ramsar sites worldwide protect an area of about 721,600 square miles (1.9 million sq. km), which is nearly the size of Mexico. Many wetland amphibians and reptiles have disappeared in recent years. Hypoxia may kill young amphibians such as tadpoles. Habitat loss also leaves these animals with fewer places to live.

Amphibians breathe oxygen through their skin. If there are pollutants in the water, the animals also absorb these in their skin. These pollutants may impair the animal's ability to swim, catch food, or reproduce. Reptiles can experience similar problems. When exposed to harmful pollutants, they may produce eggs with thinner shells and have fewer young.

The Nene Recovery Initiative works to restore the population of Hawai'ian geese.

On February 2, the Convention on Wetlands is signed in Ramsar, Iran. This day is now World Wetlands Day.

The United Nations Development Program launches the Wetlands Ecosystem and Tropical Peat Swamp Forest Rehabilitation Project in an effort to improve the world's wetlands.

President George W. Bush announces a plan to expand the no net loss policy with a promise of creating 3 million acres (12.1 million hectares) of new wetlands in the U.S.

1971   **1986**   **1990**   **2002**   **2004**   **2009**

From 1986 to 1997, approximately 58,500 acres (23,675 hectares) of wetlands are lost each year in the mainland United States. This adds up to more than 1,000 square miles (2,600 sq. km) of lost wetland ecosystems in more than a decade.

The United States government promises to protect wetlands. The new policy is based on the idea of "no net loss" of wetland ecosystems. This means that any wetlands destroyed must be replaced.

The Upper Mississippi River Floodplain Wetland becomes the 26th U.S. wetland named a wetland of international importance under the Ramsar Convention on Wetlands. The site covers an area of 472 square miles (1,224 sq. km).

Science in the Wetlands

Biologists studying birds in wetland ecosystems must go to great lengths to stay hidden from the birds they study.

To learn more about wetlands, scientists use modern technology. Some scientists use microscopes to look at animal cells. Through these cells, scientists can determine an animal's health, as well as the health of its environment. Other scientists study the growth rings of trees to see the effects of factors such as fires or hurricanes. Scientists also study the **genetics** of plants and animals, making sure there is enough diversity to keep populations strong.

Using Technology

Although most scientists spend time collecting data in wetlands, other scientists use technology to study wetlands from afar. Gathering information in this way is called remote sensing. They study satellite or aerial photographs of wetlands. These photographs show scientists the entire wetland community. Scientists can see where water is located, the types of vegetation in each area, and what areas have been flooded by incoming tides. By comparing modern and historical photographs, scientists can also see how wetlands have changed over time.

Predicting Change

Some scientists map wetlands using Geographic Information Systems (GIS). GIS provides very detailed information about wetland elements, including vegetation, soil types, and wildlife. Scientists use this information to predict what would happen to wetlands if certain elements changed. They try to discover what would happen if the amount of rainfall increased or an area flooded.

Eco Facts

Europe is home to about 5,000 constructed wetlands. The United States has about 1,000 of these wetlands.

Flat-bottomed airboats powered by airplane propellers are used to travel through swamps. They skim the surface of the water at high speeds.

Constructed Wetlands

Natural wetlands clean pollutants from water, so scientists sometimes design and build wetlands to improve water quality in polluted areas. These areas are called constructed wetlands. Constructed wetlands are less expensive to build, operate, and maintain than large wastewater treatment plants. Constructed wetlands can also adapt to changing water levels. To create constructed wetlands, a scientific team prepares the area by scooping out dirt. The team plants vegetation or allows it to grow in naturally.

Scientists sometimes use drones, or unmanned aircraft, to collect data about the atmosphere and the environment.

Working in the Wetlands

Scientists sometimes use mist nets to safely capture wetland birds for studies. Later, the birds are released.

People who work in wetland ecosystems play an important role in maintaining the health of these areas. They find ways to improve wetland habitats. Scientists also learn about the vital role wetlands play in the environment.

Marine Biologist

Duties

Studies the plants and animals that live in oceans and saltwater wetlands

Education

Bachelor of science in biological science; master's degree in marine biology

Interests

Animals, plants, chemistry, computer science, math, science, and working outdoors

Marine biologists study saltwater plants and animals. They collect data about water temperature, oxygen levels, acidity, and pollution levels. Marine biologists also study fluctuations in plant and animal populations and the relationships between species.

Other Wetland Jobs

Environmental Engineer

Seeks to control, reduce, and prevent pollution and help solve other environmental problems

Wetland Ecologist

Takes measurements to determine the health of wetland ecosystems and helps plan and implement programs that restore wetlands to their natural state

Biologist

Studies the plant and animal life found in wetlands and anything that affects the natural balance in the ecosystem

Sylvia Alice Earle

Sylvia Alice Earle (1935–) is an American marine biologist and undersea explorer. She received her bachelor's degree from Florida State University in 1955. By 1966, she had earned a doctoral degree from Duke University.

In 1970, Earle led the first all-woman team of **aquanauts**. The team spent two weeks living in an underwater laboratory to study deep sea ecosystems. Earle went on to lead more than 100 deep sea expeditions, logging about 7,000 hours under water. She also set a record for the deepest solo dive, with a depth of 3,281 feet (1 km).

During her career, Earle held many positions in numerous companies and organizations. In 1981, Earle co-founded two companies to design and build underwater exploration vehicles and robots. She became the first woman to serve as chief scientist of the National Oceanic and Atmospheric Administration in 1990.

Earle has written more than 150 scientific publications, authored 11 books, appeared in hundreds of television productions, and given scientific talks in more than 60 countries. Her work has earned her medals of recognition from scientific organizations around the world. She has also been awarded 15 honorary degrees and has been inducted into the National Women's Hall of Fame.

Underwater Viewer

Unlike some wetland creatures, people do not have a membrane that closes over their eyes so they can see underwater. Try building an underwater viewer to see beneath the surface of the water without diving below the surface.

Materials

scissors

plastic bottle

clear plastic wrap

rubber band

1. With an adult's help, use the scissors to cut the bottom from the plastic bottle. Recycle the cap or lid.

2. Cut a piece of plastic wrap large enough to cover the bottom and sides of the bottle. Place the bottomless bottle on the sheet of plastic wrap.

3. Secure the wrap to the bottom of the bottle with the rubber band.

4. Take the viewer to a nearby wetland. Hold it in the water so that only the part wrapped in plastic is underwater. Look through the top of the viewer. Do you see any plants or animals? Record your findings.

Create a Food Web

Use this book, and research on the Internet, to create a food web of wetland ecosystem plants and animals. Start by finding at least three organisms of each type—producers, primary consumers, secondary consumers, and tertiary consumers. Then, begin linking these organisms together into food chains. Draw the arrows of each food chain in a different color. Use a **red** pen or crayon for one food chain and green and blue for the others. You should find that many of these food chains connect, creating a food web. Add the rest of the arrows to complete the food web using a pencil or **black** pen.

Once your food web is complete, use it to answer the following questions.

1. How would removing one organism from your food web affect the other organisms in the web?

2. What would happen to the rest of the food web if the producers were taken away?

3. How would decomposers fit into the food web?

Sample Food Web

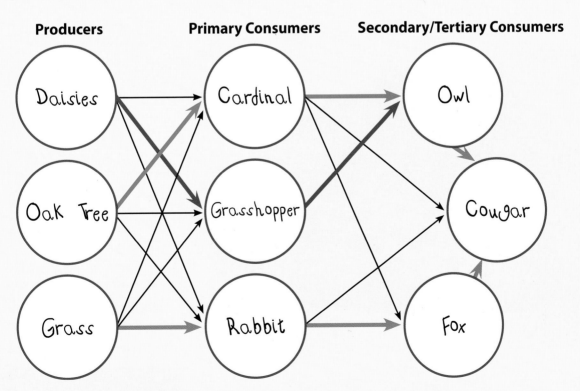

| Producers | Primary Consumers | Secondary/Tertiary Consumers |

Daisies · Oak Tree · Grass · Cardinal · Grasshopper · Rabbit · Owl · Cougar · Fox

Eco Challenge

1. What are the four types of wetlands?

2. What is the only continent that does not have wetlands?

3. What are two greenhouse gases?

4. What role do wetlands play in times of flood?

5. What are the two types of marshes?

6. How do scientists study wetland ecosystems from afar?

7. What is special about wetland plants?

8. Why do carnivorous plants eat insects?

9. Name three mammals that have adapted to living in and around water.

10. What bird was hunted nearly to extinction for its beautiful feathers?

Answers

1. Bogs, fens, marshes, swamps
2. Antarctica
3. Carbon dioxide and methane
4. They absorb precipitation, hold and store floodwater, and slow down floodwaters.
5. Freshwater marshes and saltwater marshes
6. Remote sensing
7. They can grow in water that has little oxygen.
8. They do not receive enough minerals from the water.
9. Beavers, muskrats, and otters
10. Egret

Glossary

acidic: containing acid

aquanauts: underwater explorers

carnivorous: meat-eating

deltas: deposits of sand and soil at the mouth of a river; shaped like a triangle

ecosystem: a community of living things sharing an environment

endangered: at risk of no longer existing anywhere on Earth

enzymes: proteins that perform a specific chemical reaction

fossil fuels: energy sources, such as oil and coal, that come from the remains of decomposed organisms

genetics: the study of genes or the basic units that transmit characteristics from one generation to the next

glaciers: large, slow-moving bodies of ice

global warming: an increase in the average temperature of Earth's atmosphere; enough to cause climate change

greenhouse gases: atmospheric gases that can reflect heat back to Earth

groundwater: water held below ground in rock or soil

metamorphosis: physical changes that take place during a life cycle

minerals: solid substances that occur naturally in rocks and soil

nutrients: substances that feed plants or animals

organic: made up of living things

organisms: living things

photosynthesis: the process in which a green plant uses sunlight to change water and carbon dioxide into food for itself

sediment: matter that settles to the bottom of a liquid

species: a group of similar plants and animals that can mate together

subtropical: bordering the tropics

tropical: in the tropics, an area around the equator that is hot and humid

Index

Log on to www.av2books.com

AV² by Weigl brings you media enhanced books that support active learning. Go to www.av2books.com, and enter the special code found on page 2 of this book. You will gain access to enriched and enhanced content that supplements and complements this book. Content includes video, audio, web links, quizzes, a slide show, and activities.

Audio
Listen to sections of the book read aloud.

Video
Watch informative video clips.

Embedded Weblinks
Gain additional information for research.

Try This!
Complete activities and hands-on experiments.

WHAT'S ONLINE?

Try This!	Embedded Weblinks	Video	EXTRA FEATURES
Map wetlands around the world.	Learn more about wetlands.	Watch a video about wetlands.	**Audio** Listen to sections of the book read aloud.
Find out more about animals that live in wetlands.	Find current weather forecasts in wetlands.	Watch a video about an animal that lives in a wetland.	
Test your knowledge of human activity in wetlands.	Learn how to identify different plants in wetlands.		**Key Words** Study vocabulary, and complete a matching word activity.
Write a descriptive paragraph about a day in the life of scientists working in wetlands.	Read about current research in wetlands.		**Slide Show** View images and captions, and prepare a presentation.
	Learn more about food chains.		**Quizzes** Test your knowledge.

AV² was built to bridge the gap between print and digital. We encourage you to tell us what you like and what you want to see in the future.

Sign up to be an AV² Ambassador at www.av2books.com/ambassador.